Are we there yet?

Music for Kids™

part of The Music Sales Group

London / New York / Paris / Sydney / Copenhagen / Berlin / Madrid / Hong Kong / Tokyo

CW01583021

Published by
Music For Kids
14-15 Berners Street, London W1T 3LJ, UK.

Exclusive Distributors:
Music Sales Limited
Distribution Centre, Newmarket Road, Bury St Edmunds, Suffolk IP33 3YB, UK.
Music Sales Corporation
257 Park Avenue South, New York, NY 10010, USA.
Music Sales Pty Limited
20 Resolution Drive, Caringbah, NSW 2229, Australia.

Order No. MFK100078
ISBN: 978-1-78038-556-3

Created by John Bassett.
Design and illustrations by Simon Abbott.
Music processed by Paul Ewers Music Design.
Edited by Toby Knowles.
Backing Tracks by Rick Cardinali.

Printed in China.

Are we there yet?

Sing along with
the CD!

Play the songs
at home!

Complete the travel
scenes with the stickers!

This book belongs to:

CONTENTS

Alice The Camel

Verse 2:
Alice the camel has four humps.
Alice the camel has four humps.
Alice the camel has four humps
So go, Alice, go.
Boom, boom, boom.

Verse 3:
Alice the camel has three humps.
Alice the camel has three humps.
Alice the camel has three humps
So go, Alice, go.
Boom, boom, boom.

Verse 4:
Alice the camel has two humps. etc.

Verse 5:
Alice the camel has one hump. etc.

Verse 6:
Alice the camel has no humps.
Alice the camel has no humps.
Alice the camel has no humps
So Alice is a horse!

The Ants Came Marching

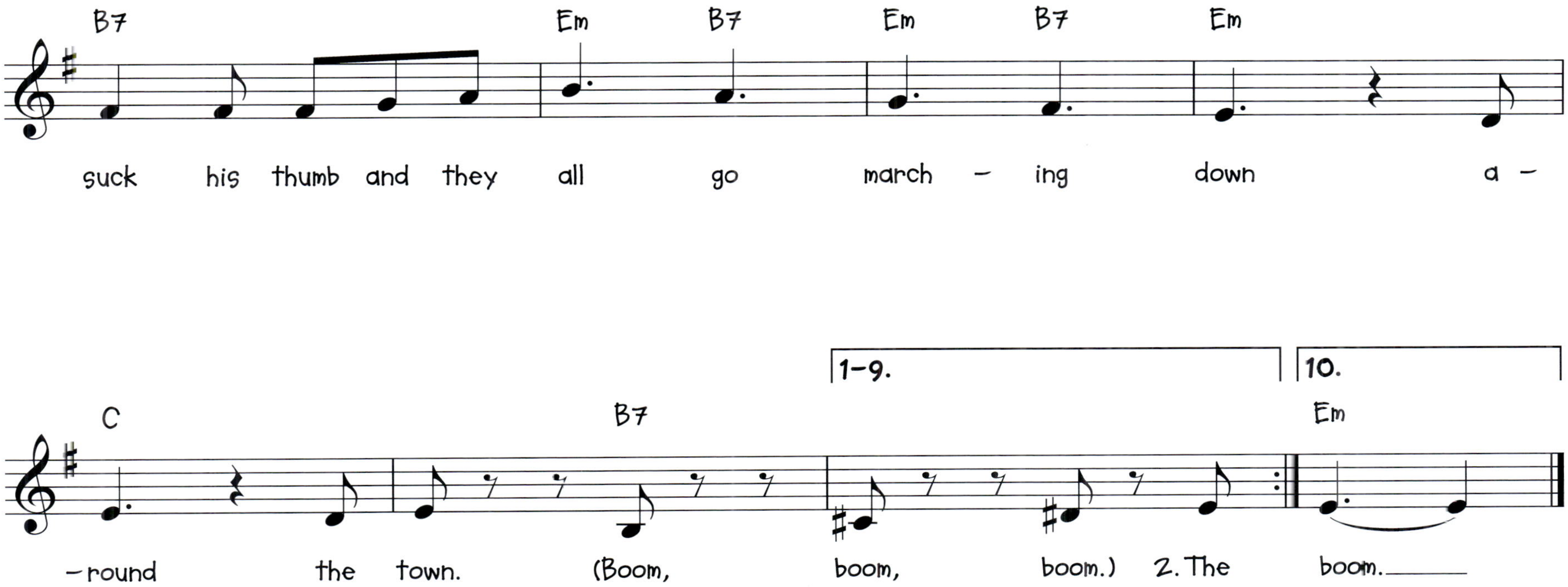

Verse 2:
The ants came marching two by two; Hurrah! Hurrah!
The ants came marching two by two; Hurrah! Hurrah!
The ants came marching two by two,
The little one stopped to tie his shoe,
And they all go marching down around the town.
(Boom, boom, boom.)

Verse 3:
The ants came marching three by three; Hurrah! Hurrah!
The ants came marching three by three; Hurrah! Hurrah!
The ants came marching three by three,
The little one stopped to climb a tree,
And they all go marching down around the town.
(Boom, boom, boom.)

Verse 4:
The ants came marching four by four...
The little one stopped to shut the door...

Verse 5:
The ants came marching five by five...
The little one stopped to take a dive...

Verse 6:
The ants came marching six by six...
The little one stopped to pick up sticks...

Verse 7:
The ants came marching seven by seven...
The little one stopped to go to heaven...

Verse 8:
The ants came marching eight by eight...
The little one stopped to shut the gate...

Verse 9:
The ants came marching nine by nine...
The little one stopped to scratch his spine...

Verse 10:
The ants came marching ten by ten...
The little one stopped to say "the end"...

Bingo

With a bounce

* As you sing through verses 2–6, replace each letter with a clap, as shown below.

Verse 2:
There was a farmer had a dog,
And Bingo was his name–o.
(Clap)–I–N–G–O!
(Clap)–I–N–G–O!
(Clap)–I–N–G–O!
And Bingo was his name–o!

Verse 3:
There was a farmer had a dog,
And Bingo was his name–o.
(Clap, clap)–N–G–O!
(Clap, clap)–N–G–O!
(Clap, clap)–N–G–O!
And Bingo was his name–o!

Verse 4:
There was a farmer had a dog,
And Bingo was his name–o.
(Clap, clap, clap)–G–O!
(Clap, clap, clap)–G–O!
(Clap, clap, clap)–G–O!
And Bingo was his name–o!

Verse 5:
There was a farmer had a dog,
And Bingo was his name–o.
(Clap, clap, clap, clap)–O!
(Clap, clap, clap, clap)–O!
(Clap, clap, clap, clap)–O!
And Bingo was his name–o!

Verse 6:
There was a farmer had a dog,
And Bingo was his name–o.
(Clap, clap, clap, clap, clap)
(Clap, clap, clap, clap, clap)
(Clap, clap, clap, clap, clap)
And Bingo was his name–o!

Five Little Ducks

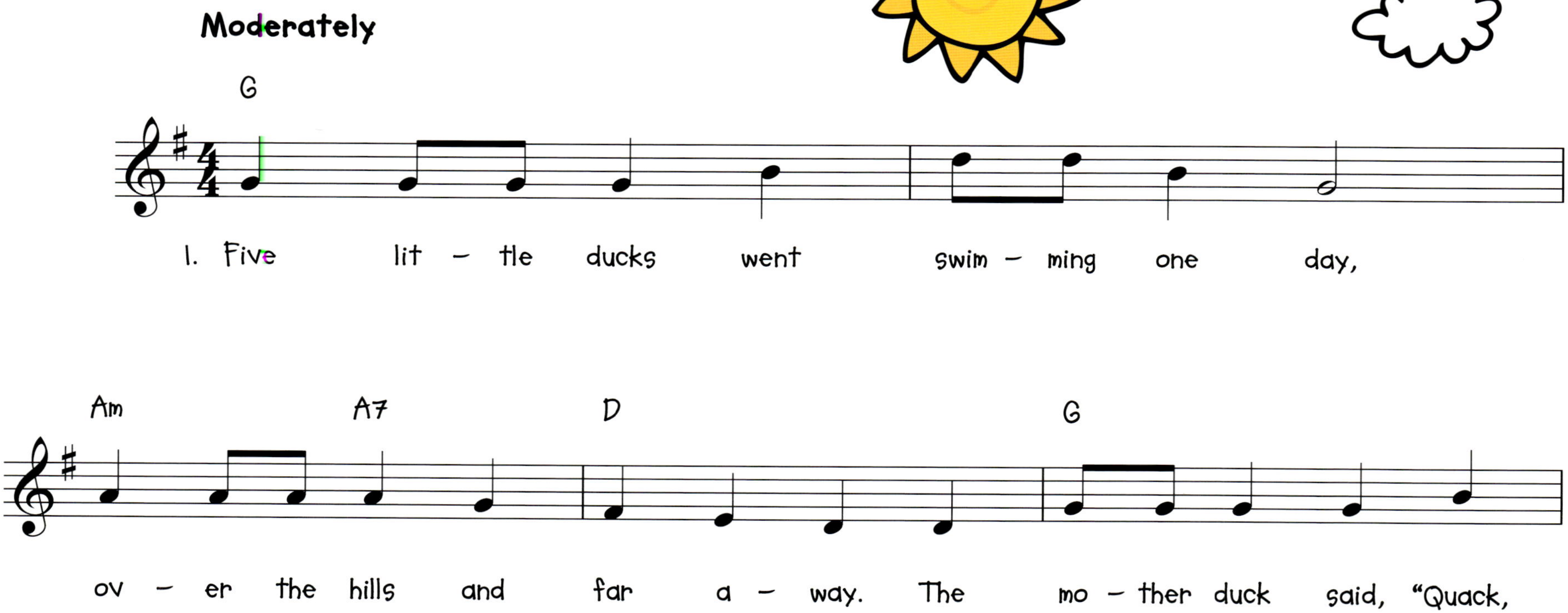

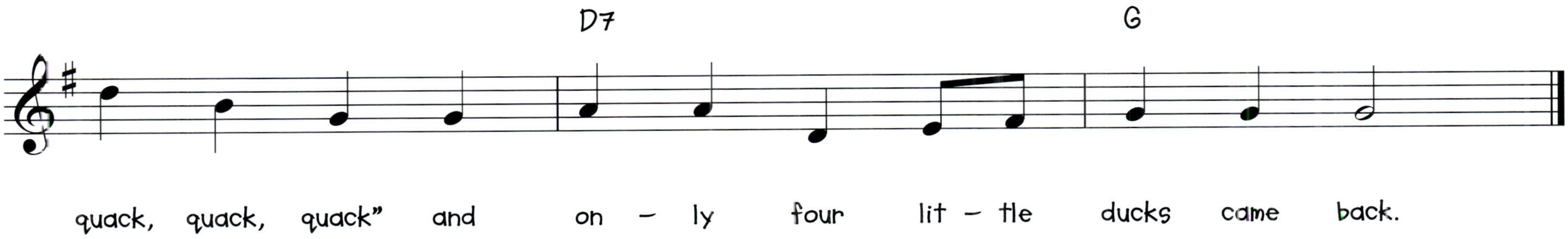

Verse 2:
Four little ducks went swimming one day, etc.

Verse 3:
Three little ducks went swimming one day, etc.

Verse 4:
Two little ducks went swimming one day, etc.

Verse 5:
One little duck went swimming one day,
Over the hills and far away.
The mother duck said, "Quack, quack, quack, quack"
And five little ducks came swimming right back.

The Grand Old Duke Of York

G
D7
when they were up, they were up and when they were down they were down, and
G
C
G
D7
G
when they were on - ly half way up they were nei - ther up nor down.

London Bridge Is Falling Down

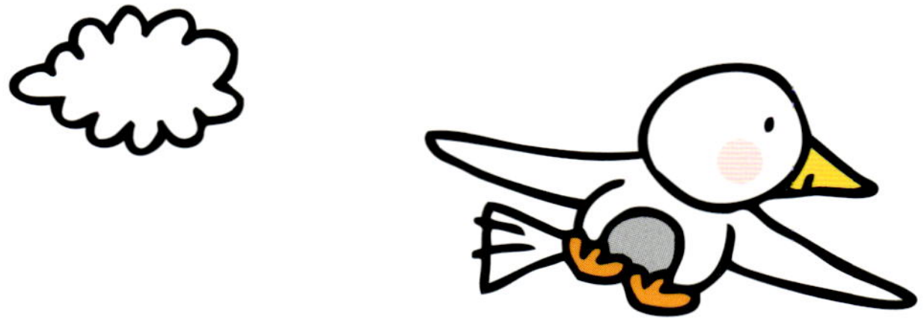

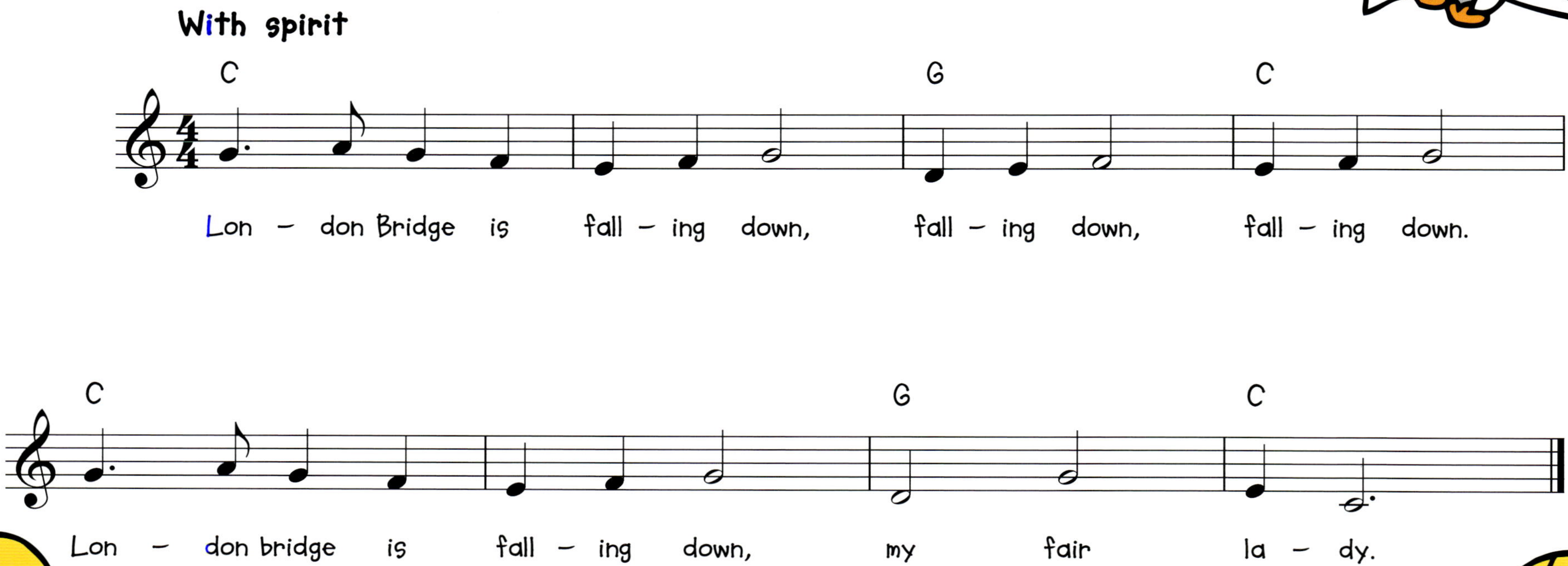

Verse 2:
How shall we build it up again,
Up again, up again?
How shall we build it up again,
My fair lady?

Verse 3:
Build it up with iron bars,
Iron bars, iron bars!
Build it up with iron bars,
My fair lady!

Verse 4:
Iron bars will bend and break,
Bend and break, bend and break.
Iron bars will bend and break,
My fair lady.

Verse 5:
Build it up with pins and needles,
Pins and needles, pins and needles!
Build it up with pins and needles,
My fair lady!

Verse 6:
Pins and needles rust and bend,
Rust and bend, rust and bend.
Pins and needles rust and bend,
My fair lady.

Verse 7:
Build it up with penny loaves,
Penny loaves, penny loaves!
Build it up with penny loaves,
My fair lady!

Verse 8:
Penny loaves will tumble down,
Tumble down, tumble down.
Penny loaves will tumble down,
My fair lady.

Verse 9:
Build it up with gold and silver,
Gold and silver, gold and silver!
Build it up with gold and silver,
My fair lady!

Verse 10:
Gold and silver I've not got,
I've not got, I've not got.
Gold and silver I've not got,
My fair lady.

Use your stickers to complete this travelling scene.

Merrily We Roll Along

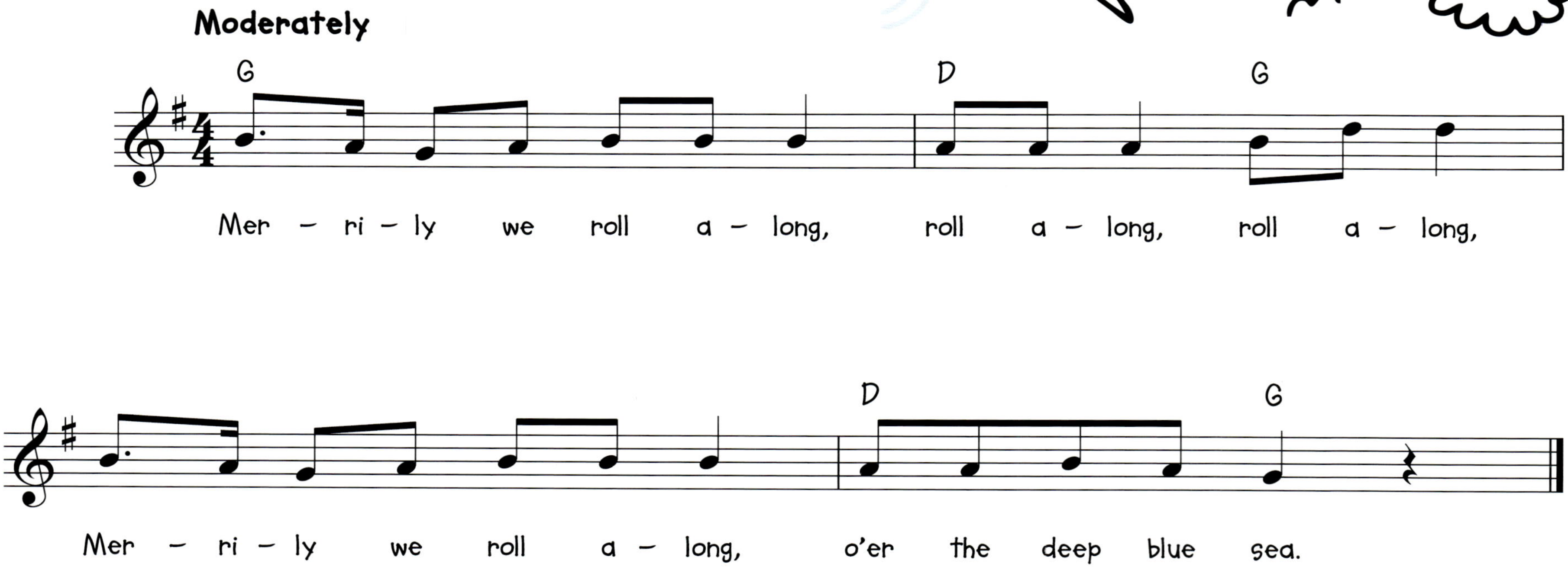

Michael Finnegan

Verse 2:
There was an old man called Michael Finnegan,
He went fishing with a pin again.
He caught a fish then dropped it in again.
Poor old Michael Finnegan, begin again.

The Muffin Man

Moderately

D G C A7 D
Do you know the Muf - fin Man, the Muf - fin Man, the Muf - fin Man? Oh,
G C D7 G
do you know the Muf - fin Man, his wares are such a treat.

Old MacDonald Had A Farm

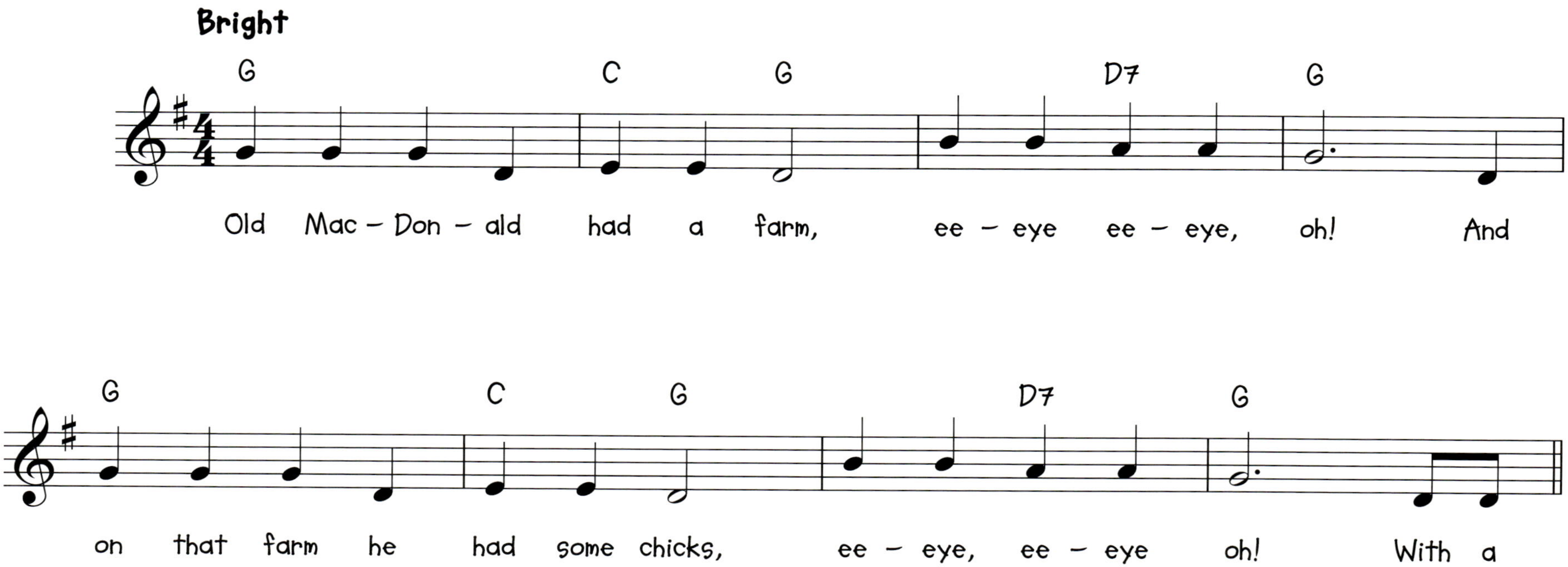

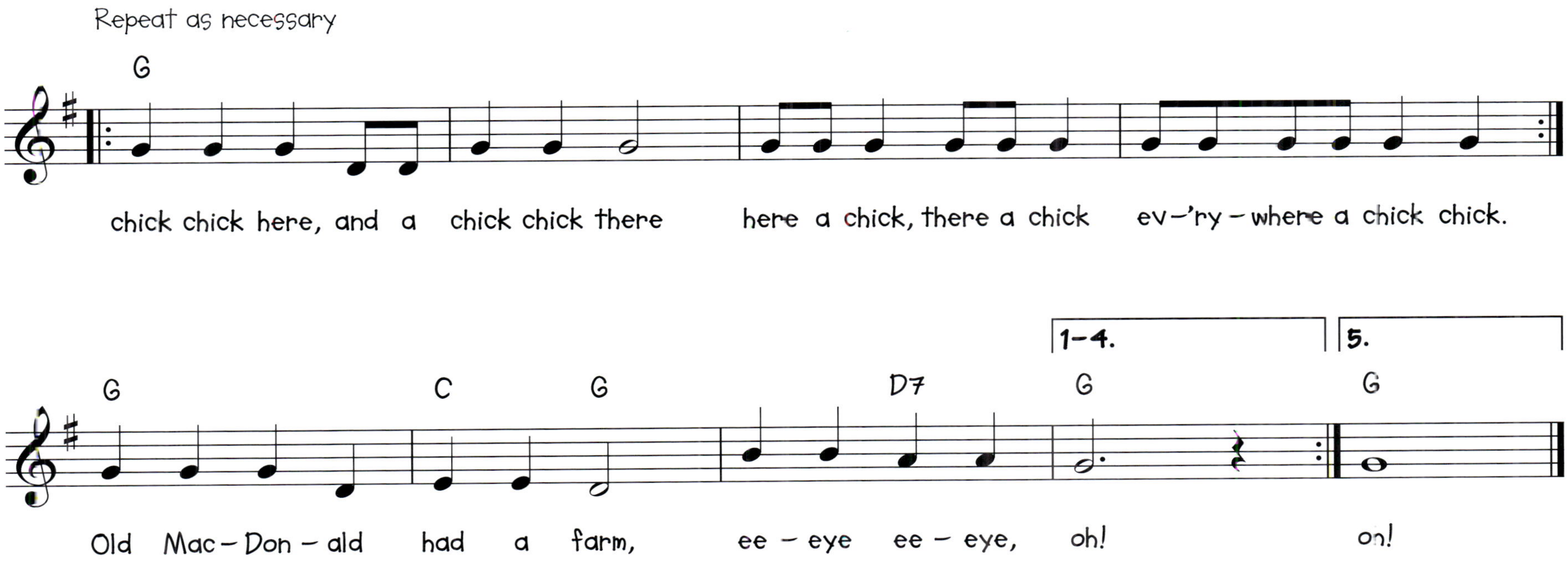

Verse 2:
Old MacDonald had a farm
Ee-eye, ee-eye, oh!
And on that farm he had some ducks,
Ee-eye, ee-eye, oh!
With a quack quack here...

Verse 3:
Cows – Moo Moo!

Verse 4:
Pigs – Oink Oink!

Verse 5:
Sheep – Baa Baa!

One Man Went To Mow

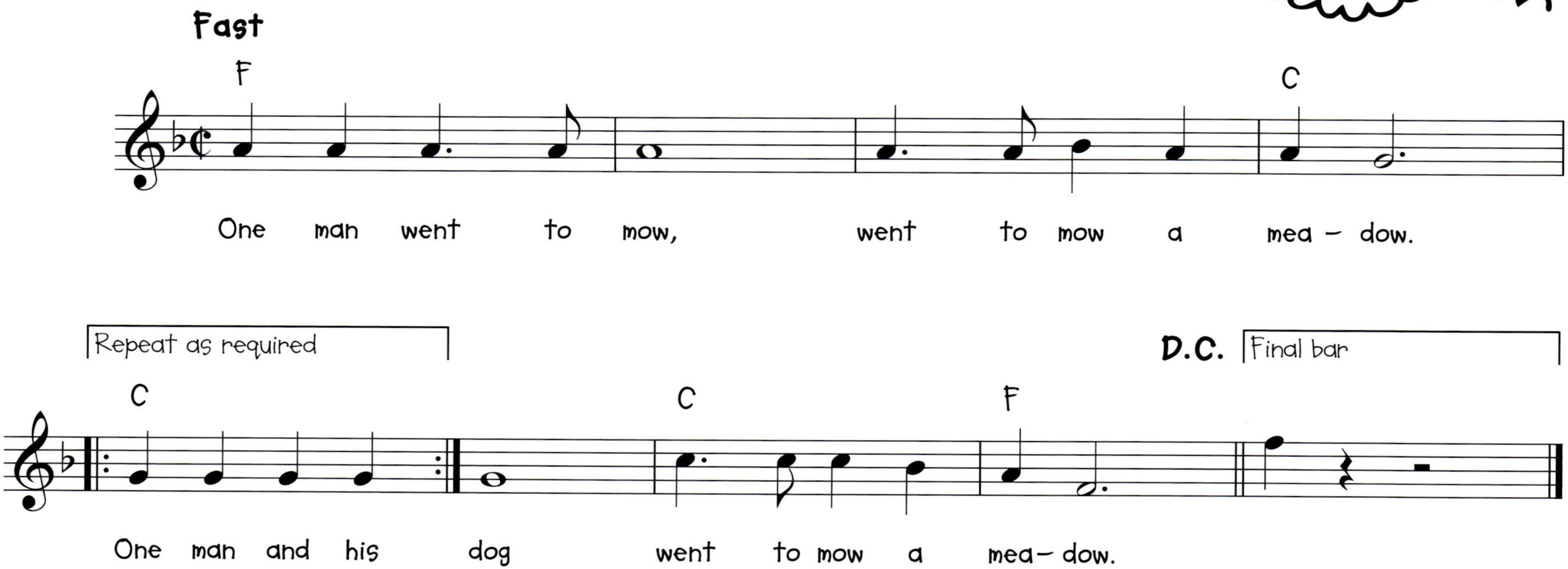

Verse 2:
Two men went to mow,
Went to mow a meadow.
Two men, one man and his dog
Went to mow a meadow.

Verse 3:
Three men went to mow,
Went to mow a meadow.
Three men, two men, one man and his dog
Went to mow a meadow.

Verse 4:
Four men went to mow, etc.

Verse 5:
Five men went to mow, etc.

Verse 6:
Six men went to mow, etc.

Verse 7:
Seven men went to mow, etc.

One, Two, Three, Four, Five

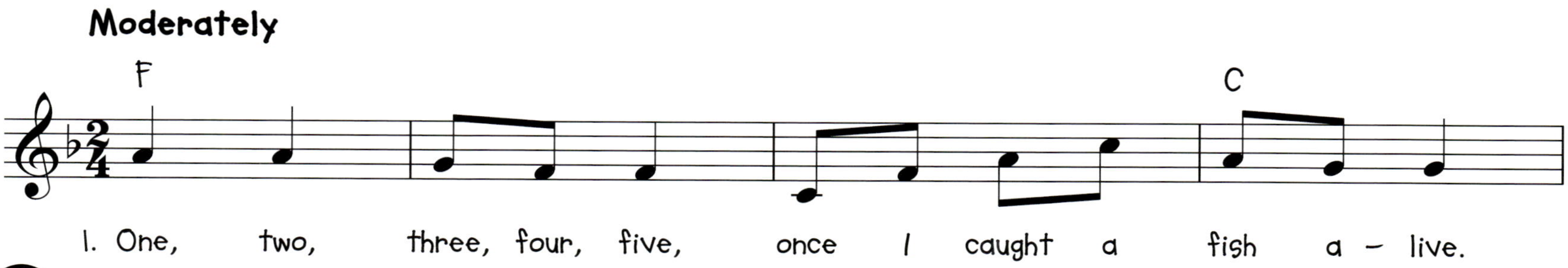

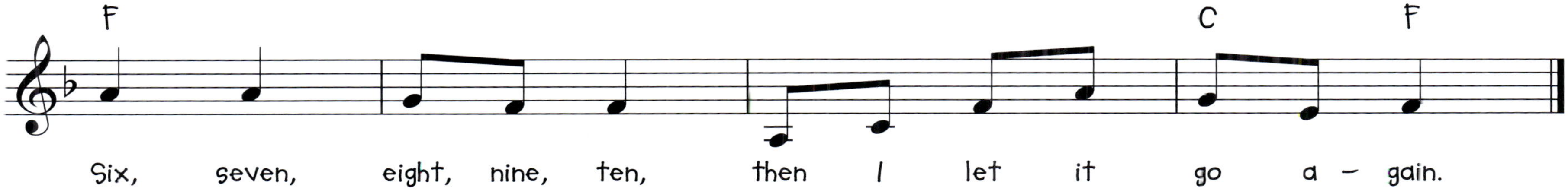

Verse 2:
"Why did you let it go?"
Because it bit my finger so!
"Which finger did it bite?"
This little finger on the right.

Use your stickers to complete this holiday scene

Polly Put The Kettle On

F Bb G C7
Su - key take it off a - gain, Su - key take it off a - gain,
F Bb C7 F
Su - key take it off a - gain, they've all gone a - way.

Row, Row, Row Your Boat

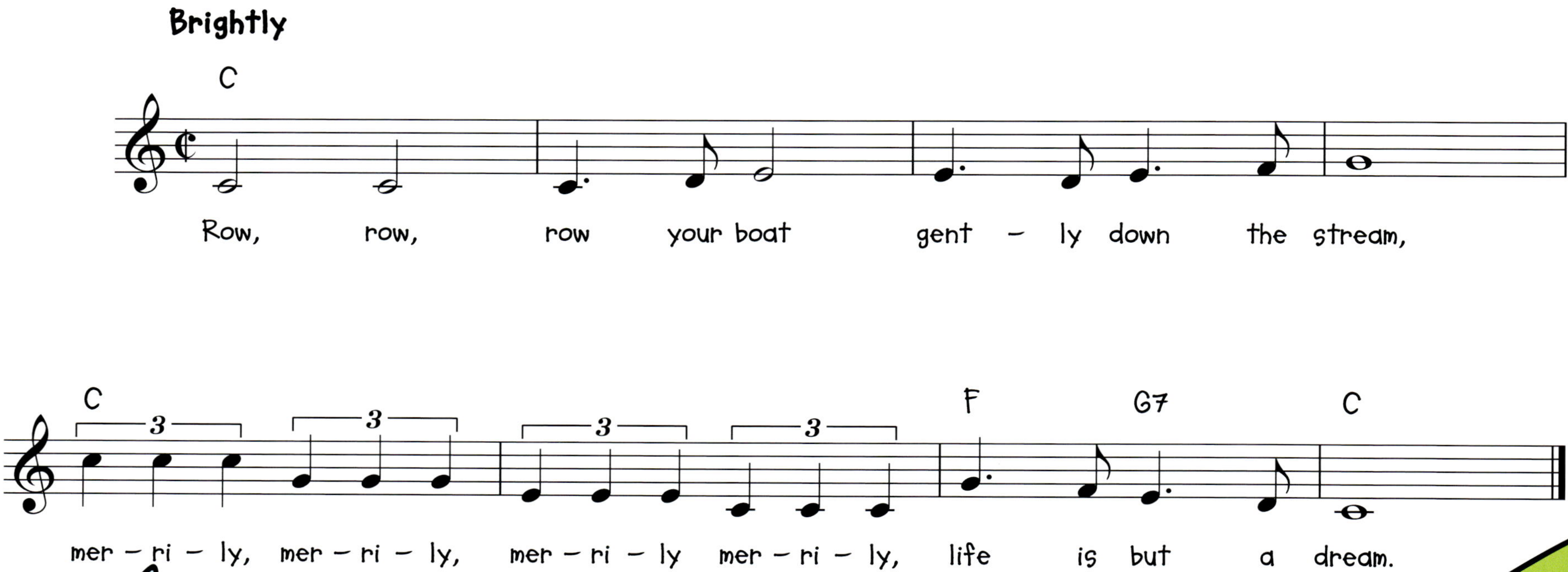

This Old Man

Moderately

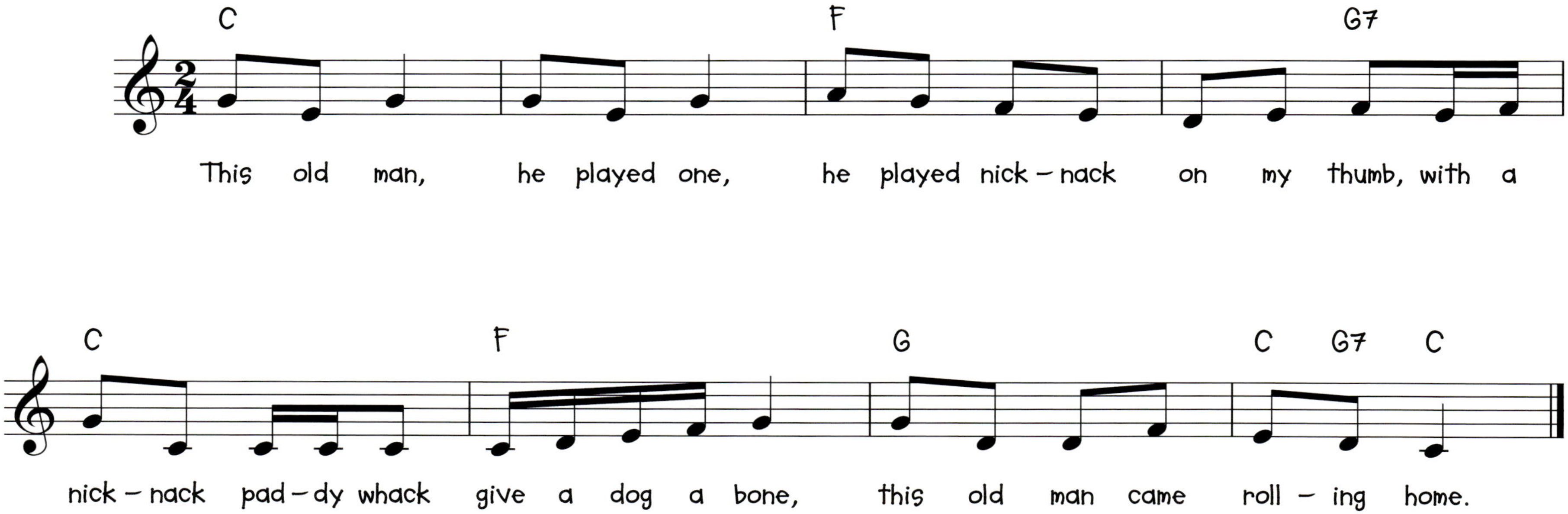

Two Little Chickens

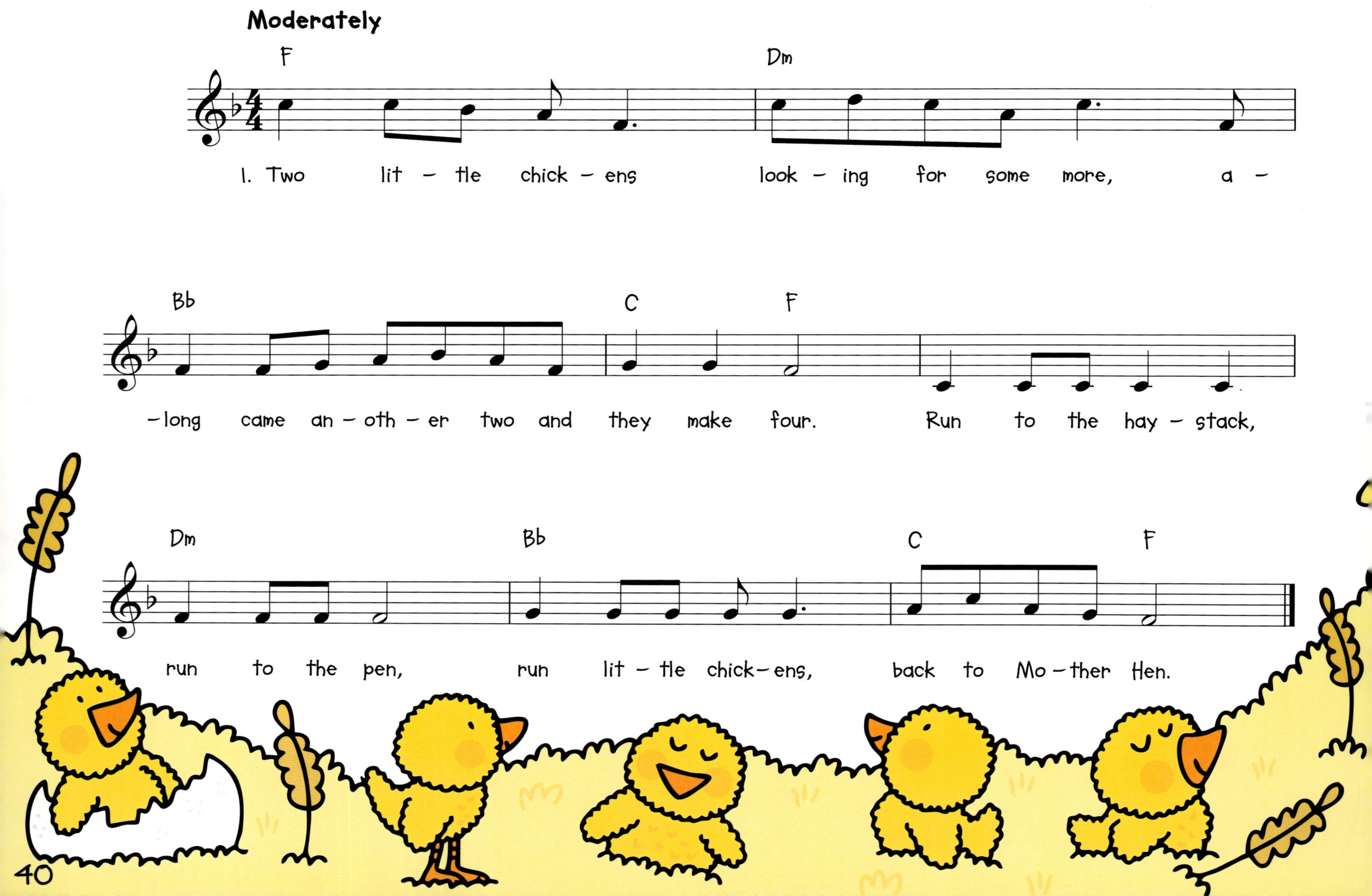

Verse 2:
Four little chickens getting in a fix,
Along came another two and they make six.
Run to the haystack, run to the pen,
Run little chickens, back to Mother Hen.

Verse 3:
Six little chickens perching on a gate,
Along came another two and they make eight.
Run to the haystack, run to the pen,
Run little chickens, back to Mother Hen.

Verse 4:
Eight little chickens run to Mother Hen,
Along came another two and they make ten.
Run to the haystack, run to the pen,
Run little chickens, back to Mother Hen.

Two Little Dickie Birds

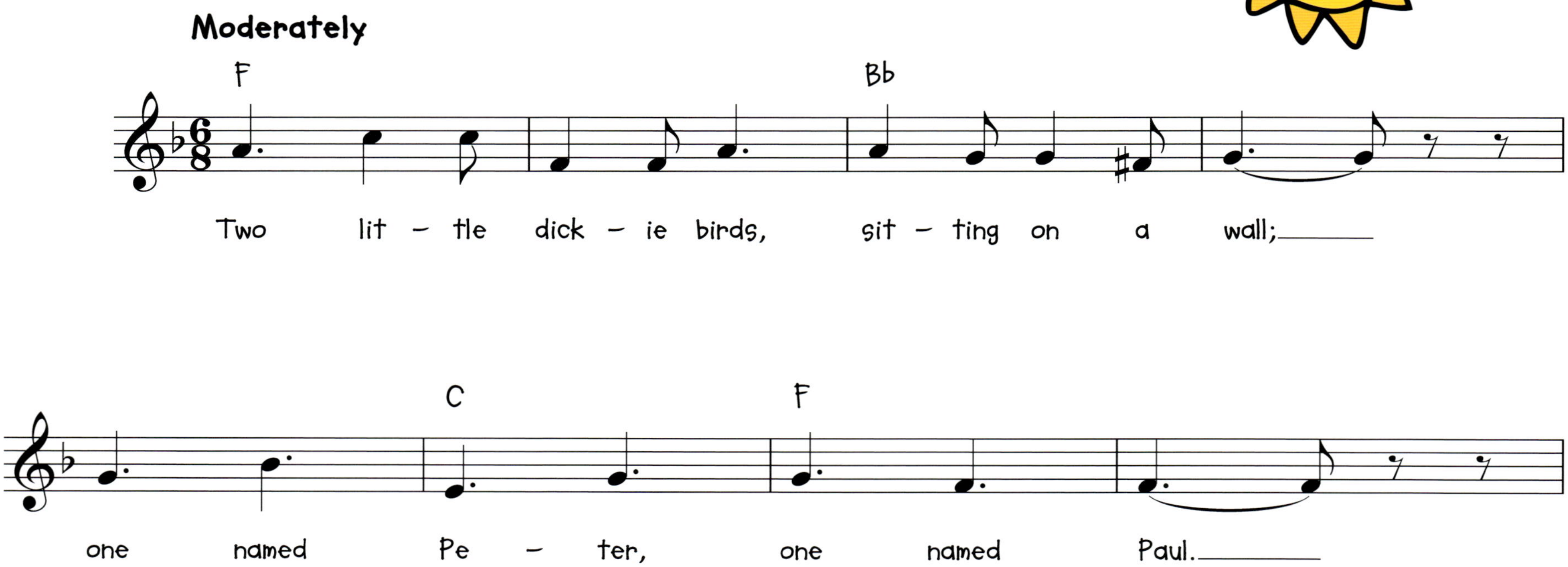

Bb
Fly a – way, Pe – ter! Fly a – way, Paul!
C F
Come back, Pe – ter! Come back, Paul!

The Wheels On The Bus

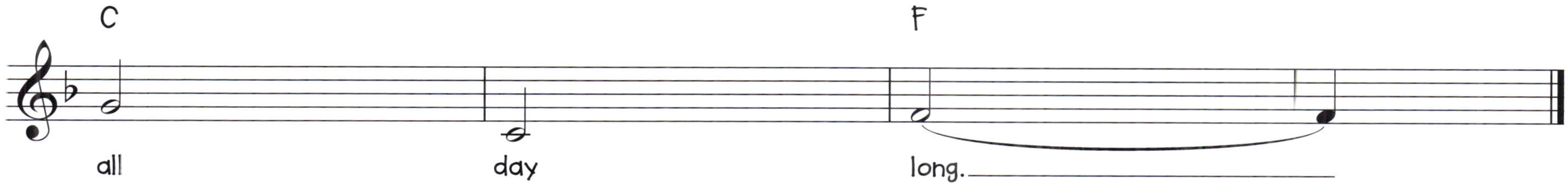

Verse 2:
The wipers on the bus go
Swish, swish, swish,
Swish, swish, swish,
Swish, swish, swish.
The wipers on the bus go
Swish, swish, swish,
All day long.

Verse 3:
The people on the bus bounce
Up and down,
Up and down,
Up and down.
The people on the bus bounce
Up and down,
All day long.

Verse 4:
The horn on the bus goes
Beep, beep, beep,
Beep, beep, beep,
Beep, beep, beep.
The horn on the bus goes
Beep, beep, beep,
All day long.

Guitar Chords

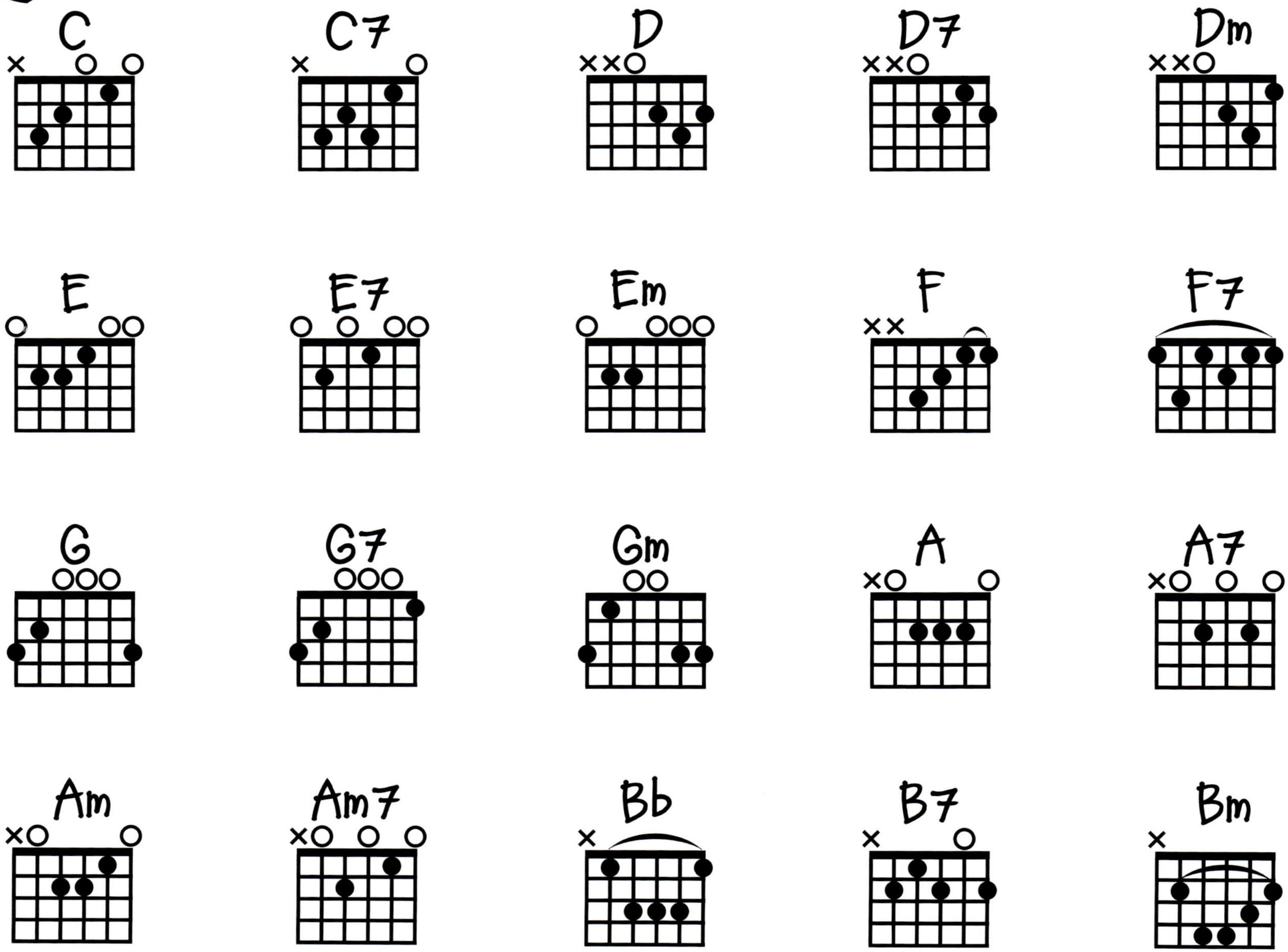

Ukulele Chords

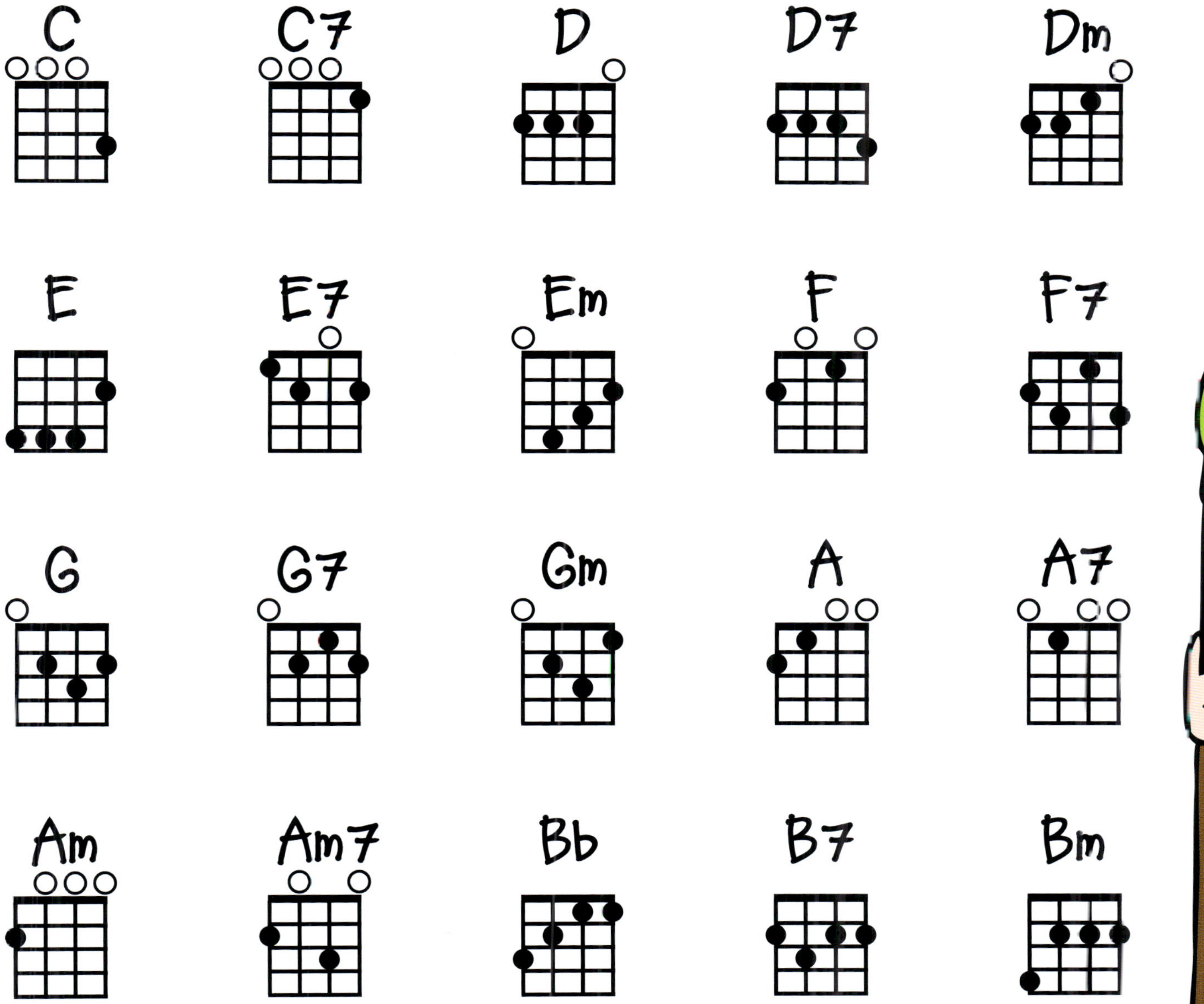

CD Track List

1. Alice The Camel
2. The Ants Came Marching
3. Bingo
4. Five Little Ducks
5. The Grand Old Duke Of York
6. London Bridge Is Falling Down
7. Merrily We Roll Along
8. Michael Finnegan
9. The Muffin Man
10. Old MacDonald Had A Farm
11. One Man Went To Mow
12. One, Two, Three, Four, Five
13. Polly Put The Kettle On
14. Row, Row, Row Your Boat
15. This Old Man
16. Two Little Chickens
17. Two Little Dickie Birds
18. The Wheels On The Bus